Cats of the World

Discover Cat Breeds and Their Countries of Origin

Rose Brown

Published by The Crackajack Company
Imprint: Brainy Bubs
Text and concept by Rose Brown
This book is intended for educational and entertainment purposes only. These animals carry the stories and spirit of their homelands, whether by history, legend, or love.
First Edition, 2026

Siamese Cat

Thailand

Did you know? Siamese cats are famous for their striking blue eyes and talkative nature.

Persian Cat

Iran

Did you know? Persian cats are one of the oldest and most luxurious cat breeds in the world.

Maine Coon

United States

Did you know? Maine Coons are one of the largest domesticated cat breeds.

British Shorthair

United Kingdom

Did you know? British Shorthairs are known for their chubby cheeks and calm personality.

Bengal Cat

United States

Did you know? Bengal cats have wild leopard-like spots but are completely domestic.

Scottish Fold

Scotland

Did you know? Scottish Fold cats have unique folded ears that make them look like owls.

Sphynx Cat

Canada

Did you know? Sphynx cats look hairless but actually have a soft peach-like fuzz.

Russian Blue

Russia

Did you know? Russian Blue cats are known for their plush silver-blue coat.

Norwegian Forest Cat

Norway

Did you know? These cats are built for cold weather with thick double coats.

Egyptian Mau

Egypt

Did you know? Egyptian Maus are one of the few naturally spotted cat breeds.

Turkish Angora

Turkey

Did you know? Turkish Angoras are known for their silky white fur and elegance.

Abyssinian Cat

Ethiopia

Did you know? Abyssinians are one of the oldest known cat breeds.

Turkish Van

Turkey

Did you know? Turkish Vans love water—rare for cats!

American Shorthair

United States

Did you know? These cats were originally brought on ships to catch mice.

Birman Cat

Myanmar

Did you know? Birmans have beautiful blue eyes and white "gloves" on their paws.

Ragdoll Cat

United States

Did you know? Ragdolls go limp like a ragdoll when picked up.

Devon Rex

United Kingdom

Did you know? Devon Rex cats have curly fur and huge ears.

Cornish Rex

United Kingdom

Did you know? Cornish Rex cats have only one layer of soft curly fur.

Japanese Bobtail

Japan

Did you know? These cats have short, bunny-like tails.

Chartreux

France

Did you know? Chartreux cats are known for their quiet and gentle nature.

Siberian Cat

Russia

Did you know? Siberian cats are strong and can survive harsh winters.

Tonkinese Cat

Canada

Did you know? Tonkinese cats are a mix of Siamese and Burmese breeds.

Ocicat

United States

Did you know? Ocicats look wild but have no wild DNA at all.

Balinese Cat

United States

Did you know? Balinese cats are long-haired versions of Siamese cats.

Havana Brown

United Kingdom

Did you know? Havana Browns are known for their rich chocolate-colored coats.

Loved this book?
Discover more fun and learning with other titles in the Did You Know series, each with a companion coloring book, brought to you by The Crackajack Company.

9 788169 067652

Printed at Repro India Ltd.